ERWIN

A Life From B

Copyright © 2017 by Hourly History Limited

All rights reserved.

Table of Contents

Introduction
Building the Next War
Rommel Trains the Rabble
Rommel's Return to War
The Desert Fox
The Fox Makes his Rounds
Against All Odds
Near Death Experience
A Choice is Made
Mislaid Plans
Rommel Takes the Fall
Conclusion

Introduction

Johannes Erwin Eugene Rommel was born on November 15[th,] 1891 in the city of Ulm in southern Germany. Ulm has a rich history, and the settlement of the region itself can be traced all the way back to 7000 years ago when Neolithic pioneers roamed the countryside. The incarnation of this ancient European dreamscape that Rommel was born into was then known as the Second German Empire, or as it referred to in German, the "Deutsches Reich."

The first German Empire or Reich was the Holy Roman Empire, a conglomeration of Central European states that lasted for nearly 1000 years before being dismantled by Napoleon Bonaparte in 1806. This Second German Empire, or Reich, on the other hand, only had a shelf life that lasted from 1871 to 1918, when it disintegrated at the closing of World War One.

This Second Reich would only last for a few decades, and its utter collapse was a humiliation for many German's sense of pride. This was acutely the case with Erwin Rommel as well. At the close of World War One, he was a Captain of the German Army Corps, and, like many officers he felt betrayed by the leadership of the new German government, most especially the "Treaty of Versailles" that had, with the signing of a pen, reduced the once robust German army into a minuscule force of only 100,000 men.

This stripping of the military sent those in the profession into a state of complete shock and dismay. The younger generation of officers, such as Erwin Rommel, had a distinct feeling that they had somehow been betrayed or possibly even tricked into such a disastrous surrender. Many considered that if they had kept on fighting on into 1919 that the outcome would have been somehow different. This common sentiment of betrayal that Rommel and many of his fellow officers shared at the closing of World War One would one day be exploited to its fullest extent by yet another veteran of the conflict, Rommel's future commander-in-chief, Adolf Hitler.

Chapter One

Building the Next War

"Don't fight a battle if you don't gain anything by winning."

—Erwin Rommel

After the virtual implosion of German society at the end of World War One, many looked to the returning officer class to restore order from the chaos. Erwin Rommel was now just barely 27 years old, but he had acquired much more experience than his youthful face belied. Returning to Lucia Maria Mollin, the wife he had married in November 1916 during the height of the war, Rommel seemed at first to be content with a quiet civilian life, settling down in Stuttgart, Germany.

However, by the summer of 1919 Rommel was on the move again, sent to train a special internal security group in Friedrichshafen, an old industrial city located on the shore of Lake Constance in the south of Germany. Here, Rommel, the impeccable soldier, found men that were extremely undisciplined and with a seeming refusal to obey commands from their superior officers. Rommel was given the task to drill these unruly men into shape.

The men initially lambasted Rommel with insults and mockery, refusing to listen to reason. This prompted Rommel to hold an emergency meeting with the rambunctious recruits, in which he famously stood on top of a desk and yelled to the rabble rousers that he was there to "command soldiers, not criminals." The next day, Rommel led the men some distance from their sleeping quarters when they once again began to give him trouble and refused to follow instructions, Rommel simply jumped on his horse and sped off, leaving them all behind.

After the group finally managed to walk back to their barracks, their will to disobey had been broken, allowing Rommel to mold them into the men he wanted them to be. The local Chief of Police came a few days later to check up on the job that Rommel was doing and is said to have been so impressed by the quick turnaround that he offered Rommel an official job with the police department.

The life of the beat cop was not for Erwin Rommel; instead, he went back to the same regiment he had known since joining the army in 1910. With foreign battles far behind him, the main directives given to Rommel during the interwar years were to train the men under his charge not as wartime soldiers but as a quickly assembled force of riot police, ready to squash any domestic disturbance or civil disobedience that the discontented German citizenry seemed to be plagued with in the post-World War One years.

Instead of fighting glorious battles against foreign aggressors, Rommel now had to fight his own people. It is not a prospect that he relished, but being the dutiful soldier that he was, he usually followed his orders. Wishing to avoid spilling the blood of his fellow countrymen if it was at all possible, he would often lean more toward negotiation than force, a tendency that was indicated when he was charged to retake the city of Lindau, which had been overrun by revolutionary communists.

Not wishing to create a bloodbath by marching on the city, Rommel instead opened up a channel with the city's council and found a way to retake it through diplomacy rather than force. Such actions won Rommel much admiration, and he was viewed as a voice of moderation in the midst of the chaos and upheaval that often surrounded him in the wrecked social and political systems of post-war Germany.

Despite his restraint, Rommel could see the very real threats that Germany was facing both inside and out. Like many of his contemporaries, he feared a communist takeover more than anything else. World War One, after all, had been the catalyst that helped the Russian revolutionary Vladimir Lenin convert Russia into a communist state, and many of his Bolsheviks were indeed eyeing Germany as the next capitalist domino to fall in the post-war wreckage.

The idea of classless hordes of communists taking over his country was utterly appalling to an upper-class officer such as Erwin Rommel, and he intended to do everything he could to stop a Russian-styled October Revolution from occurring in Germany as well, spending the next decade suppressing one communist uprising after another, including the infamous "Bavarian Soviet Republic" in which communist revolutionaries seized control of Munich, Germany, attempting to break away completely from the recently established Weimar Republic.

These events greatly troubled Rommel and made him view national solidarity in the face of such threats with increasing importance. These views he took with him when he was assigned as an infantry instructor in Dresden, in 1929. From 1929 to 1933 he would teach a new generation of recruits rising up out of the wreckage of the First World War, even as they prepared for the building of the next.

Chapter Two

Rommel Trains the Rabble

"Sweat saves blood; blood saves lives, but brains save both."

—Erwin Rommel

Despite the constant upheaval in the German system during the interwar years, Erwin Rommel and his wife Lucia lived a fairly pleasant life, with all the luxury that Rommel's salary as a commissioned officer could provide. They even managed to take a few vacations, including one in 1927 that took the Rommel's to Italy, in which Erwin recounted some of his battles at the very same locale.

Thinking his overseas military exploits were long behind him, this was mostly just introspective wistfulness on his part. Rather than the outbreak of war, the next major event in Rommel's life was the birth of his only son, Manfred, on December, 24th 1928. He would spend the next four years as an infantry instructor until he was promoted to the rank of Major in 1933.

An even more major event occurred that very same year that would change everything in Rommel's hitherto boringly benign existence: the election of Adolf Hitler. Rommel, like many of the career soldiers of his day, was mostly oblivious to the political undertakings of the German government; when Hitler came to power on January 31st, 1933, Rommel barely even batted an eye.

Even though there can be no doubt that he was alarmed by some of the political unrest that he saw, like many other officers of his era, he still thought it was much more prudent just to follow his orders as they came and stay out of politics altogether. According to the later testimony of Rommel's wife, he was rather ambivalent about Hitler, but while other officers may have shown disdain for the formal corporal from Austria seizing power.

Rommel simply viewed Hitler as an idealist with a patriotic mission to save Germany from external and internal threats that the nation faced. He didn't have much of a problem with the idea of Hitler, but according to his wife, he did have a great disdain for much of Hitler's followers, especially the notorious "Brownshirts," or as they were officially known, the S.A., a Nazi paramilitary group, which Rommel viewed as simply a bunch of undisciplined and uncouth bullies.

This was the general opinion of most of the German military's High Command as well, a sentiment that prompted Hitler—who did not yet have full control of the military—to rein in his most loyal but ruthless followers. This is what led to the "Night of the Long Knives" on June 30th, 1934 in which nearly 100 S.A. members were left dead in a sudden purge of their ranks.

Hitler, with no love lost for those that had helped him gain power in the first place, readily discarded the loyalty of his most devoted followers in favor of greater leverage with Germany's core group of military officers. Hitler's official explanation of the sudden liquidation was that certain members of the S.A. had been plotting a coup to overthrow the German government.

Rommel, like many other officers, readily accepted this explanation without much more thought about it, and life, for the most part, went on as usual in the Rommel household. It was about one year later, on October 15th, 1935, that Rommel received his new post orders and was sent off to be an instructor at the War Academy in the city of Potsdam, right next to the neighboring German capital of Berlin. He lived there in modest housing with his wife and young son, where they attempted to soak up some

Berlin social life whenever Rommel could get away from his teachings at the Academy.

During this time, Rommel continued his disdain of the Nazis, and even though he had to some extent grown to admire Hitler, he still did not care much for many of his followers. Much to his chagrin, as the year 1935 drew to a close, it was in this perplexed condition that he was given his next assignment; he was ordered to train and oversee the S.A. The very group of rabble-rousing bullies and thugs he so often loathed, he was now expected to train officially.

Rommel did not look forward to such a task but, just as he did so many times before, he saw it as his duty to straighten out the S.A. rabble. He carried on like this for the next three years until his stint at Potsdam came to a close on November 9th, 1938, and as a result of his service, Rommel was now a full-fledged Colonel.

At this time in his life, it is believed that Rommel may have resented the fact that most of his rising through the ranks was occurring during peacetime since most professional soldiers of the day relished the chance to prove their merit in actual war. However, Erwin Rommel would not have to wait much longer for his wartime opportunity to arise when just a few months' later events in Poland would finally spark the Second World War.

Chapter Three
Rommel's Return to War

"In a man-to-man fight, the winner is he who has one more round in his magazine."

—Erwin Rommel

Right on the eve of the German invasion of Poland, Rommel received another promotion, this time to General. The invasion then began in earnest on September 1st, 1939 when a joint force of German troops in the west and Soviet troops in the east simultaneously invaded the Polish nation. It is a strange irony that two political ideologies that were supposed to have nothing but anathema for each found themselves suddenly working in collusion to tear Poland apart.

This was all the result of the secret German/Russian Non-Aggression Pact that had been signed just one week prior, which had laid the groundwork and given the green light for such an audacious venture. Even though half of Poland was being occupied by Soviet communists with at least what amounted to the temporary blessing of his Fuhrer, Rommel, for the most part, viewed the German role as one of liberation, freeing the Polish people from communist agents and agitators.

No matter what the circumstances were, he made himself believe in the mission. As he would later describe to his wife, Rommel purported that "the inhabitants drew a breath of relief that we have arrived and rescued them." Regardless of what the average Polish person may have felt, the rest of the world certainly did not take such matters lightly. After many months of appeasement, the international community had finally had enough of Nazi Germany.

Britain and France led the charge, and both of them immediately declared war on Germany after the Polish invasion. Erwin Rommel was sent to the front lines of France. May 10th 1940 was the start date of the official invasion, and Rommel was soon leading a group of Panzer divisions up the Meuse, a major river that runs through France and Belgium.

Once they arrived at the riverbanks, they found that they could not cross, since all of the bridges had been destroyed. Rommel then struggled to find a way for his men to cross but was beaten back by French artillery aimed at them from the opposite side of the river. In order to overcome these obstacles Rommel strategically placed his own tanks and artillery in order to create cover for his men. He then went so far as to set the nearby houses on fire (regardless of what the residents may have thought about it) in order to create an elaborate smoke screen.

With as much cover established as possible Rommel then finally had his infantry brave the expanse in a series of rubber boats. It was here that Rommel's boldness truly came forth, because even while his men were hesitant at the prospects of jumping into a river under heavy French machine gun fire, Rommel led the way in grand fashion. It is said that he was so enthusiastic that he picked up his own machine gun and started firing at the French before jumping down into the water to stabilize pontoon bridges for his troops.

After all of this struggling, Rommel's men managed to cross to the other side. The tank divisions then followed, led by Rommel himself. The Panzers now made their rapid advance, beating back much of the French counterattack, but the next morning Rommel himself would nearly meet his end when his tank became stuck in a sand quarry. How ironic for the man who would later be known as the Desert Fox of North Africa to nearly meet his demise in a miserable little sand trap in France!

As he struggled to free himself, things did not look good for Rommel at all. Soon he was bombarded with heavy anti-tank rounds, blasting right into the hull of his tank, completely disabling it. A group of French infantry then charged forward attempting to grab their prize, but Rommel was rescued at the last minute by another German tank commander, Colonel Rothenburg, who used his own tank to scatter the French infantry who were attempting to capture Rommel.

After this near disaster, Rommel's unit pushed on without much incident eventually reaching the French town of Cateau, where his men managed to completely annihilate the French II Army Corps, taking as many as 10,000 French soldiers prisoner, and only losing 36 men in the process. This blitzkrieg-styled victory was then followed up by several more until on June 19[th,] 1940 Erwin Rommel personally accepted the surrender of the French leadership.

An armistice with the French was then signed just a few days later on June 22[nd,] making France annexed German territory. It was a giddy and exciting time for many of Germany's generals, Rommel included, that their arch enemy from World War One, the French, had been so easily defeated.

Chapter Four

The Desert Fox

"Democracy is beautiful in theory; in practice it is a fallacy."

—Benito Mussolini

With the French subdued, Rommel turned his attention to a new front in the war, this time in North Africa. Being appointed the commanding officer of the Deutsches Afrika Korps, in charge of the 21st Panzer Division, he arrived in Tripoli, Libya on February 12th, 1941. Libya was supposed to be the domain of another Axis power; Italy, but the forces of Benito Mussolini had been recently all but crushed by the British.

In desperate need of support, Rommel and the Afrika Corps were sent to intervene. It was here in the North African sands that Rommel earned the nickname the Desert Fox. As soon as Rommel arrived on the scene, he was a man of action. He didn't have much time to get to know all of the men whose training and direction he was taking over but he made sure they knew who he was as he began intensively drilling them in his own theories of tactics and tank warfare, as well as sharing his recent real-life experiences in Poland and France.

Although Rommel was technically supposed to play a subordinate role to Italo Gariboldi, the main Italian general on the ground, Rommel would frequently resort to covert acts and even outright insubordination if he felt the war effort was not going in the direction that he wished. Rommel's main problem with the Italian leadership was that he felt that they were simply taking too long and wasting too much time in getting back on the offensive with the British.

From Rommel's point of view, Germany had just gone to great lengths to bolster the struggling Italian force, but rather than use this strengthened army to retake the momentum from the British, the Italian leadership stagnated and remained indecisive. Prompting Rommel to take matters into his own hands, the German general then launched his own offensive against the British in Libya on March 24th with a German division flanked by two Italian divisions.

It was precisely due to Rommel's brazen disobedience to the official pronouncements of the Italian leadership that he managed to catch the British completely off guard. British forces had been relying upon intelligence reports that indicated Rommel was ordered to remain in place until early May, making the British truly believe that no attack would occur for a few more months.

Little did these intelligence experts know that Erwin Rommel, the Desert Fox, was more than ready to disobey these orders. To make matters worse for the British, thinking that they were not in any immediate danger, three whole divisions that had previously been stationed in North Africa had been temporarily relocated to the war effort in Greece. As a result of these mishaps, the British were defeated, and the Libyan town of Mersa El Brega fell to Rommel in just one day.

Rommel's men then charged on to the infamous town of Benghazi, forcing the British to evacuate the city quickly. Despite the fact that Rommel had achieved in just a matter of days what the Italian troops had failed to do in months, the Italian generals were furious that Rommel had not stayed in position as he was asked to do. A few days later a message arrived from German General Franz Halder that actually echoed the Italian sentiment and advised Rommel to listen to the Italian commanders.

As crafty as ever, when General Gariboldi asked Rommel what the message was all about, Rommel, knowing that Garibaldi didn't know the German language, lied about its contents, and told Gariboldi that the message from General Halder gave him permission to take charge and do as he pleased. Amazingly, General Gariboldi believed this outrageous lie and immediately acquiesced to General Erwin Rommel.

Now firmly in control, Rommel would then go on to lead an attack on the British garrison in the Libyan port city of Tobruk. Being a port with open access to the Mediterranean, Tobruk was of vital strategic importance to the British, allowing them to bring in endless supplies and reinforcements through the port. Rommel wanted to have this advantage for himself, knowing that he could greatly increase the ability of his supply lines to keep up with the demands of his army.

Before it was overrun by the British, this city had previously been a strategic Italian fortress, helping to secure Italian territorial ambition in Libya for about 30 years. After the British takeover it was filled with divisions of British, Australian, and even Indian infantry, creating a combined force of about 35,000 soldiers. Due to such concentrated force, the Allied fighters were able to repel several Axis attempts at reclaiming the fortress.

Ultimately Rommel would not be able to take the city of Tobruk until June 20th, 1942. For his efforts Rommel managed to take 32,000 allied fighters prisoner, acquired a huge cache of weapons and supplies, and gained a vital port for the war effort; on June 22nd, in recognition of his success, Rommel was promoted to the rank of General Field Marshal. This time, the Desert Fox was not going to be outdone.

Chapter Five
The Fox Makes his Rounds

"It's good to trust others but, not to do so is much better."

—Benito Mussolini

After the fall of Tobruk, Field Marshal Rommel wanted to keep momentum on his side and not allow his Allied opponents a chance to gather reinforcements. At this point in the war effort, Rommel was absolutely certain that the best course of action would be to drive a series of tank divisions right into the heart of Egypt and take them all the way to Alexandria before seizing the Suez Canal. This North African version of the blitzkrieg would place most of the African Mediterranean under German control.

Rommel believed that such decisive blows to British holdings in the region would break the back of the Allied effort. Back in Germany, however, Adolf Hitler had other plans, and with Tobruk secure, refused to send Rommel any further support. Unable to gather enough manpower for a larger scale invasion, Rommel then settled on a smaller prize just 150 miles west of Alexandria: the Egyptian seaport of Mersa Matruh.

Battling another combination of British, Australian, and Indian troops, Mersa Matruh eventually fell on June 29th, 1942. Among the spoils for Rommel's men were barrels of gasoline and hundreds of British tanks and trucks, which were immediately put to use in Rommel's army. With his enemies on the run, Rommel then continued to drive the British back, this time to another desert fortification in the town of El Alamein, continuing straight ahead on his course, now just 66 miles west of Alexandria.

The first major battle of El Alamein commenced on July 1st, 1942. At the outset of the conflict Field Marshal Rommel had a fighting force of over 100 tanks, but despite the size of his armored division, the Allies dominated the air, and under relentless bombing runs, Rommel's tanks found themselves in constant peril as slow moving targets trapped in the desert. Rommel would vainly continue his advance over the next few days, but the domination of Allied airpower continually beat his divisions back.

By July 14th Rommel's army was struggling, barely holding off infantry attacks, and even getting stuck in horrible sandstorms. Rommel would eventually regroup, however, and launch a new attack on August 30th, this time at Alam el Halfa, just south of El Alamein. Here Rommel wished to pull the British into an attack that would overextend their line, allowing Rommel to cut off and surround them.

One of the major problems with this strategy, however, were the countless minefields that had been laid down right in the general vicinity of Alam el Halfa. As if active minefields were not bad enough, Rommel's armored divisions also had to worry about getting stuck in hidden spots of quicksand that were ready to suck tanks straight to the bottom of the desert.

Due to all of these circumstances, Rommel found his army unable to outflank the British, and by September 2nd, realizing that defeat was inevitable, Rommel was forced to organize a strategic withdrawal. At the end of the battle of Alam el Halfa, Rommel's forces had been depleted of 2940 men and 50 tanks, as well as numerous miscellaneous weapons and transport vehicles that now littered the smoking ruin of the desert.

Along with these material losses, Rommel himself had also been physically drained, and becoming dangerously ill from a bad liver infection coupled with low blood pressure, he was evacuated by air back to Germany in order to receive treatment. Immediately before being admitted to the hospital he had another appointment he had to make first with Adolf Hitler. During the meeting, Rommel personally debriefed Hitler on the latest happenings of Libya and Egypt, and the two discussed the status of their objectives in North Africa.

Despite all of his recent losses, Rommel was insistent that his Panzers were on the very brink of reaching Alexandria, but they would not be able to take the city unless they were given adequate reinforcements and supplies. Rommel informed Hitler that above all else, tank divisions needed fuel. As Rommel explained it to him, they couldn't crash down the gates of Alexandria if they ran out of gas.

In this exchange, to allay Rommel's concern, Hitler is reported to have commented, "Don't worry. I mean to give Africa all the support needed. Never fear, we are going to get Alexandria all right." Hitler then informed Rommel that Germany was just now in mass production of especially suited small landing boats that could carry fuel without being quite as easily targeted as the large oil tankers that were being sunk in the Mediterranean on a daily basis.

Hitler told them that these smaller boats were much more capable of for refueling maneuvers and were even armed with two 88 mm guns for protection. In reality, these crafts were just recent prototype inventions that were barely off the drawing board; there was no way they could be in service, let alone be mass produced, anytime soon. It appears that Hitler was feeding Rommel a bit of an exaggeration, to say the least.

Among other things Hitler also let slip that his scientists were busily working on a new bomb that as he put it, "would throw a man off his horse at a distance of over two miles" from where the bomb was dropped. Rommel was a bit more incredulous with this tale from Hitler, but as it turns out, Hitler was referencing the nascent Nazi efforts to create an atomic bomb - a program that would later be cut for projects that provided faster results.

Along with these less tangible developments, Hitler personally took Rommel out to a tank factory and showed him the latest Tiger tanks coming off the assembly line. Hitler then reassured Rommel that North Africa would be given top priority for these new tanks. These reassurances at first worked to buoy Rommel's spirits, but his confidence was short lived when Hitler suddenly announced that he didn't want Rommel to return to North Africa after all but would instead be handed over to the Army Group in the Ukraine.

Despite all of his talk of helping Rommel succeed in Africa, Hitler claimed that he was concerned with Rommel's health and felt that a "change of climate" would be good for him. After Rommel had checked into the hospital for treatment, Hitler would change his mind once again, however, when he received word that Rommel's replacement in the field, General Stumme, had unexpectedly died of a heart attack.

Desperately needing someone capable in the field to replace him, on October 24th, 1942, Hitler personally called Rommel on the hospital telephone to ask him to return to North Africa. Rommel was still in no condition to fight, but his long obsession with coming out on top in the desert sands of Africa would not let him refuse. Against doctor's orders, Rommel checked himself out of the hospital the very next morning and caught the next flight out.

Chapter Six
Against All Odds

"A risk is a chance you take; if it fails you can recover. A gamble is a chance taken; if it fails, recovery is impossible."

—Erwin Rommel

Upon his return to the African front, the battle seemed to have already been lost before he had arrived. Rommel was horrified by the condition of his armored divisions. Everyone seemed to be perpetually running out of fuel on a continual basis. As much as he looked for them, the new oil boats Hitler had told him about were nowhere to be seen, and the regular oil tankers weren't doing much better.

Thanks to British intelligence, the Allies knew about every new Axis shipment in advance, and due to their dogged interception and bombardment, only a small percentage was actually getting through to Rommel's divisions. Making the situation even worse, Italian dictator Benito Mussolini was virtually hoarding all the supplies the Italians had, stockpiling them in Tripoli and refusing to send them to Rommel.

The sheer scarcity of Rommel's resources completely forced him off the offense and into a more defensive mode, just to be able to conserve the little fuel they had, greatly altering his tactics in his next attempt to take El Alamein. Rommel had to conserve fuel until just the right moment, and that moment came on October 26th when he led his last tank charge on El Alamein. It was a valiant effort on Rommel's part, but the charge was quickly knocked back by British artillery and aerial bombardment.

This was then followed up by a vicious ground assault led by an Australian infantry division. Outgunned and outnumbered, things now looked completely hopeless, and by November 3rd, 1942, Rommel's Afrika Korps began their retreat. This retreat was then challenged by Adolf Hitler himself when he sent a direct order for them to "fight to the last man."

Rommel would eventually refuse this order. However, deciding it better to salvage as much of what was left of his men in a tactical retreat. With only about 80 German tanks left in the face of six hundred pursuing British tanks it was not an easy task to achieve, and by all accounts, the British should have been able to outflank and encircle his retreating force.

On November 6th, fate would intervene on Rommel's behalf when a heavy downpour of rain suddenly struck, turning the previously dry desert into vast tracts of mud, greatly slowing down the British advance. After a struggle, Rommel was finally able to make it all the way to Tunisia where he was able to regroup. His arrival coincided with the first deployment of U.S. troops in nearby Morocco.

Soon after, Rommel would engage in his first battle with American soldiers, managing to deliver a decisive defeat even with a much smaller army. Rommel, the Desert Fox, would continue to evade and strike out against his much larger foes over the next few months until he finally returned to Germany once again on March 9th, 1943. Without Rommel, the entire North African campaign would eventually collapse completely on May 13th, 1943.

A couple of months later after the complete disintegration of the Afrika Korps, on July 25th Rommel was on the move again when he was sent to bolster troops stationed in Greece. It would turn out into the shortest post he ever had when he was sent back to Berlin the very same day after Hitler received word of the overthrow of Italian dictator Benito Mussolini.

In a panic, Hitler sent Rommel to command a new regiment in northern Italy. Shortly after his arrival, the partisans who had overthrown Mussolini began making overtures toward the Allies for an armistice. The Germans then quickly executed a campaign to disarm the Italian forces. With the Italians pacified, Rommel was then sent on to Normandy in France to prepare for the next major Allied invasion.

Rommel's main consultant in this effort was Gerd von Rundstedt, the man whom Hitler had appointed Commander-in-Chief of the West. In surveying their options of staving off an Allied invasion, Rundstedt confided in Rommel that he felt that it was impossible to halt an Allied advance too close to the beachhead due to the immense reach of the Allies' naval artillery.

Rundstedt felt it would be best to have all German resources and armor moved further inland in order to mount a better defense. Rommel, on the other hand, was convinced that the best chance of defense that they had was to vigorously fight the Allied invaders as soon as they landed on the beach, driving them back into the ocean. In the end, it was Rommel's strategy that won out.

Rommel personally oversaw the improvement of fortifications along the "Atlantic Wall" starting in January of 1944. Drawing upon his boyhood dreams of being an engineer, Rommel got to work designing some of the most impressive mine networks, tank traps, and other defensive measures that he could muster all over the beaches and fields of western France.

As eager as Rommel's ambition was, he found himself rushing to meet deadlines. He had already promised Hitler in April the entire fortification would be finished by May, but in reality, some parts of the Atlantic Wall's defenses were still in progress even when the Allies landed. Rommel himself noted in a letter written on April 22ⁿᵈ, "My inspection tour of the coastal sectors shows that unusual progress has been made. However, here and there I noticed units that do not seem to have recognized the graveness of the hour and some who do not even follow instructions. There are reports of cases in which my orders that all minefields on the beach should be alive at all times have not been obeyed."

Rommel then went on to further stress the gravity of the situation by adding, "I give orders only when they are necessary. I expect them to be executed at once and to the letter and that no unit under my command shall make changes, still less give orders to the contrary or delay execution through unnecessary red tape." Rommel was appalled by the corrupted bureaucracy that had made something as simple and clear cut as fortifying the Atlantic Wall unnecessarily delayed through bureaucratic "red tape."

When Rommel was in North Africa, whatever he told his men to do, they did it. Now, in western France, he found that his orders were sometimes changed by subordinates if not outright ignored. Nevertheless, despite such bureaucratic hurdles, preparations continued to be made. In the end, despite all of his warnings of preparation, it was perhaps Rommel himself who was caught off guard.

In fact, on the actual day of the Allied invasion on June 6ᵗʰ, 1944 Rommel wasn't even in the country, leaving Fortress France behind in order to celebrate his wife's birthday. Birthday celebrations would have to be put on hold, however, as Field Marshal Rommel was sent scrambling back to the Western Front for the fight of his life.

Chapter Seven
Near Death Experience

"In the absence of orders, go find something and kill it."

—Erwin Rommel

As Rommel worked feverishly in his last minute preparations on the Atlantic Wall, he put his boyhood ambitions to be an engineer to good use. Rommel was responsible for creating all kinds of booby traps and fortifications along France's Atlantic Wall. Some of his trademarks were wooden beams driven into beaches with land mines on top of them, waiting for an unfortunate Allied soldier to step on them.

He had boards with simple steel blades fastened to their ends littered across the beach, jutting out at odd angles, ready to slice open the less vigilant Allied soldier. Rommel also had mines placed strategically in blocks of concrete all over the beachhead as well as mines in random logs, hoping to trip up the GI's that stumbled upon them, with the blast taking out a few other soldiers with them.

The work was gruesome, but Rommel prepared such drastic measures with stunning precision. At one point in his planning, Rommel even suggested that the top secret VI Rockets—a primitive kind of ballistic missile—should be used to fire upon the region of southern England, in order to do damage to the Allies while they were still in the process of disembarking their invasion force.

Fortunately for the Allies, however, VI production had stalled, and it was deemed not worth the effort. The main objective of

Rommel's defense was to prevent the Allies from ever gaining much of a foothold on the shore of Normandy, but by the end of the night on June 6th, the Allies had landed around 150,000 troops and had already secured five different beachheads. Despite the fierce defense that Rommel had implemented, the Allied soldiers kept on driving forward.

At this point, in the face of such a massive force, Rommel determined that it would be better for his defenders to engage in a small-scale retreat so that they could regroup and then re-engage the allies as a stronger fighting force. A week later on June 17th, Rommel would then propose to Hitler this very plan. Hitler, however, not wishing to give even an inch, refused to entertain the notion.

No matter how much Hitler ignored the reality on the ground, however, as June turned into July, the situation was only getting worse. As the days wore on, the attacks by the Allies grew more and more brazen, so much so that on July 17th, 1944, when Rommel was coming back from a meeting, the car he was riding in was shot up and strafed by an Allied fighter plane.

A quite common occurrence at this point in the Allied invasion of the western front, Rommel had witnessed several vehicles being obliterated by Allied bombers during the course of the drive. Still, he never imagined that his own car would be next on the list of annihilation. Rommel's driver had tried desperately to get them out of range of the Allied plane's bombs and guns, but after a 20 mm artillery shell managed to blow off the chauffer's left arm, the car crashed, and Rommel was thrown out.

His injuries consisted of several scrapes and cuts on the left side of his head and three major fractures in his skull. Rommel's unconscious body was sprawled out in an open field when the Allied planes began to swoop down again for another attack. The men with him then scrambled to get Rommel out of this prone position and rushed in to carry Rommel out of harm's way. Rommel was completely covered in blood, much of it coming from a gash by his left eye and out of his mouth, from which it continued to spill out until Rommel was finally taken to a local Catholic hospital in which a French doctor stopped the bleeding and dressed his wounds.

The attending physician then gave a grim prognosis and told those present to prepare for the worst, declaring that Rommel didn't have much of a chance of survival. His loyal associates, however, refused to give up hope, and seeking a second opinion gathered up the still-unconscious Rommel and drove him to an Airbase hospital about 25 miles away in Bernay, France.

Here the doctors documented Rommel's severe injuries, noting a fracture at the base of his skull, two more fractures in his forehead, with his left cheekbone completely shattered, along with a wound to his left eye. Despite these grievous wounds Rommel would recover, but as a result, at one of the most critical moments during the war, Rommel would be laid up in the hospital once again.

Chapter Eight
A Choice is Made

"The battle is fought and decided by the quartermasters, long before the shooting begins."

—Erwin Rommel

In the summer of 1944, the Allied invasion of Normandy was in full swing, led by American General George Patton, and was smashing right through all of Field Marshal Rommel's carefully laid defenses. In light of such advances Rommel was once again forced to accept an inevitable defeat, yet when he tried to explain the obvious ascendancy of his opponents, his Fuehrer, Hitler would have nothing of it.

Rommel had actually sent a detailed analysis directly to Hitler just two days before his accident in which he stated, "The position on the Normandy front is becoming increasingly difficult and is rapidly approaching its crisis." Field Marshal Rommel was one of the very few of Hitler's generals who was bold enough to bring him bad news and argue against the leader's methods. Many other men had been executed just for daring to go against Hitler's directives.

Despite Rommel's opposition to Hitler's strategy, Rommel was a man that he actually respected, and would even allow himself to argue with to a certain extent, rather than just shutting down Rommel's dissent outright. Even so, when Rommel sent his tidings of doom to Hitler, the dictator was no longer in the mood for debate and, just like he had done in North Africa, Hitler was determined to see every last man fight to his death. Rommel's opinion of Hitler began to change completely.

Instead of making excuses for him and blaming all of the regime's excesses on Hitler's unruly followers and Nazi underlings, Rommel began to blame Hitler himself. He now came to the realization that Hitler could care less about the German people; for him, they were just simple fodder for his ambition. Rommel understood that Hitler would allow thousands of soldiers to perish needlessly just because his vanity couldn't stomach the words "strategic retreat."

With the curtains finally lifted from his eyes, now Rommel knew all too well the kind of man he was dealing with. Realizing just how unfit Hitler was for leadership, in the heart of Erwin Rommel there now stirred the strong desire to see Hitler removed from command completely. At the moment, these were just feelings and inclinations buried deep in Rommel's mind, and he would not dare to speak of them to anyone.

At the same time, however, a few other political dissidents, including the Mayor of Leipzig and the former Colonel-General Beck were speaking very intently about just such things, and when their conspiratorial discussion came to just who would be popular, charismatic, and capable enough to take Hitler's place they always mentioned Erwin Rommel by name as a prime candidate.

These two conspirators then reached out to the Mayor of Stuttgart, Dr. Karl Strolin, and intended to use him as a point of contact with the Rommel family. Strolin had actually known Rommel since the days of World War One when the two served together in 1918. The two had been friends ever since and still maintained periodic contact with each other.

Strolin had most recently initiated contact again, through Rommel's wife as an intermediary, in August of 1943. Strolin himself was about as bold of a detractor as you could find in Nazi

Germany, and just a few days prior to reaching out to Rommel, he had been bold enough to send a letter directly to the "Ministry of the Interior" in which he demanded that the "persecution of Jews and of Churches be abandoned" and that "civil rights be restored."

Most would have been immediately rounded up by the secret police for such daring statements, but the Mayor of Stuttgart had just enough popular support behind him that he was simply warned to "keep quiet." Despite the stonewalling, however, Strolin was at least now confident that there was currently no way to exact change through normal legal channels; it was at this point that Strolin himself had determined that the only way to change anything would be to eradicate Hitler.

Giving a copy of his dissenting letter to Rommel's wife, she promptly handed the missive to her husband and informed him of Strolin and the other conspirators' intentions. Staring at Strolin's demands for justice, and hearing of their plans, the secret longings that Rommel held deep in his heart now solidified into a solid course of action. Everything now seemed clear. There were two choices: either the destruction of Germany or the destruction of Adolf Hitler. Rommel chose the latter.

Chapter Nine
Mislaid Plans

"No plan survives contact with the enemy."

—Erwin Rommel

According to Strolin, Rommel had pledged to lend his full assistance to the plot of assassinating Hitler as early as February 1944. Although Rommel now heartily agreed that Hitler needed to be removed, in the beginning, he insisted that he shouldn't be killed but put on trial for his crimes instead. It was in this that Rommel hoped he could make the German people aware of the kind of criminal Hitler was, and in a sense lift some of the collective guilt from the average German by placing it where he felt it belonged: squarely on a condemned Adolf Hitler's shoulders.

Regardless of Rommel's desire to bring Hitler to justice and make him stand trial, such a feat at that time would not have been possible. In the end, it was determined that the only way to quickly get rid of Hitler would be to sneak a bomb into one of his meetings and blow him and other members of the Nazi leadership to smithereens.

So it was that the July 20th bomb plot had been conceived. Known as "Operation Valkyrie," this effort was led by Claus von Stauffenberg, a man who had served with Rommel's Afrika Korps during the North African campaign, during which he was severely wounded, losing his eye, his right hand, and two fingers of his left hand. Like Rommel, Claus was a firm believer that Hitler was ruining Germany, and the only hope they had was to remove him from power as quickly as possible.

No easy feat, the assassination of Hitler had already been tried a few times before. Somehow Hitler always managed to slip out of the traps laid for him. Several months before the July 20th attempt, a bomb had been placed on one of Hitler's planes, but inexplicably, the bomb failed to detonate and was later found and discarded. In another instance conspirators sought to shoot their leader at a special dinner he was attending, but after reports that Hitler was wearing a bullet proof vest surfaced, the would-be assassins lost their nerve and called off the attempt.

This time, however, the plotters were determined to make their plan work. In this Stauffenberg was their go-to man, and when he was appointed as chief of staff at the Reserve Army Headquarters in Berlin, enabled to attend Hitler's military conferences, Hitler was now directly within his reach. The conference Hitler was to attend the fateful day of the bombing began at 12:30 pm; as soon as it commenced, Staufenberg immediately excused himself to the bathroom where, unseen by the others, he prepped his bomb.

He took out a pair of pliers and used it to break the detonator of his plastic explosive, allowing a solution of copper chloride to begin dripping into the wiring of the firing pin mechanism of the bomb. Once this wiring was completely severed the bomb would go off, in effect creating a crudely constructed time bomb. Stauffenberg had two of these bombs, but when he reached to begin prepping the second, someone began pounding on the door informing him that the meeting was about to start.

Running out of time and settling on just one bomb for the Fuhrer, Stauffenberg discarded the second and placed the sole primed bomb into his briefcase and stepped into the conference room, getting as close to Hitler as possible and placing the briefcase bomb under the table. A few minutes later Stauffenberg then received a prearranged phone call and used it as an excuse to leave the room.

Exactly what happened next is not entirely clear, but it has been said that one of the colonels in attendance, a man named Heinz Brandt who had been standing near Hitler, shoved the briefcase out of the way, scooting it up under one of the legs of the conference table - a move believed to have saved Hitler's life, with the table managing to deflect much of the blast away from Hitler.

Colonel Brandt himself was not so fortunate, and one of his legs was completely blown off in the explosion. He later died from this serious injury. Hitler himself was left with a pair of shredded trousers and a perforated eardrum but otherwise unscathed. Ironically Rommel was still recovering from his own injuries from the July 17th strafing incident that had occurred 3 days prior when he heard the news of the plot's failure.

Rommel was greatly disheartened to hear of Hitler's unbelievable luck and the continual failure of the conspirators to lay a hand on him. However, Rommel would soon have much more to worry about, when, in the aftermath of the bomb blast, pieces of the conspiratorial wreckage would lead right back to Field Marshal Erwin Rommel.

Chapter Ten

Rommel Takes the Fall

"There is one unalterable difference between a soldier and a civilian; the civilian never does more than he is paid to do."

—Erwin Rommel

Immediately after the failed assassination attempt on Hitler on July, 20th, a massive effort was launched to find the conspirators. Due to the conspirators' own confusion as to the results of the bombing, it didn't take the Nazi authorities very long to find some of their main suspects, starting with General Carl-Henrich Von Stulpnagel, one of the main collaborators in the plot.

In the immediate aftermath of the failed attempt, Stulpnagel erroneously believed the outcome to be a success, and thinking Hitler was dead he then issued an edict to arrest the Gestapo and other secret police units. Stulpnagel would very quickly realize his mistake, however, when the next day he was ordered to report to the Army Headquarters in Berlin.

Fearing interrogation and torture at the hands of the secret police he had just ordered to be arrested, in the middle of his drive to Berlin he asked his driver to pull over, stepped out to a nearby canal, and shot himself in the head. Amazingly Stulpnagel survived the gunshot wound, and his driver found him and pulled him from the water. He then took the general to a nearby hospital; where, delirious with pain, he began to talk about Rommel, instantly implicating Rommel in the plot to kill Hitler.

The surgeon who operated on Stulpnagel immediately reported what he had heard to the Gestapo. After his surgery, Stulpnagel was then whisked away to Berlin where he was tortured and eventually killed. The Gestapo meanwhile took note of all the intelligence information they had gathered from Stulpnagel and soon made good on following up these leads.

After all of the rumbling and intrigue that implicated Rommel, it was only on September 6th that he was formally suspended from his duty as Chief of Staff. Then, on September 27th, Hitler's henchman Martin Bormann informed Hitler that all of the captured conspirators had implicated Field Marshal Erwin Rommel in the plot, resulting in the Gestapo sending secret police to put Erwin Rommel under immediate surveillance.

The Field Marshal was then ordered to report to Berlin for a special conference on October 10th to "discuss his future employment." Rommel, realizing that after all of the intrigue surrounding him, and after having so many open disagreements with Hitler, knew it probably wasn't a promotion that the Nazi government had in mind for him; he knew that the news would not be good.

Knowing this, and also being simultaneously advised by his doctors that his health was not in good enough shape to make the trip, Rommel refused to go. The next day on October 11th, after during a visit by the German Admiral Friedrich Ruge, Rommel doubled down on his reasoning for staying home, telling the Admiral, "I shall not go to Berlin. I would never get there alive."

The Admiral at first assumed Rommel was referring to his deteriorating health, but Rommel then clarified his statement by adding, "I know they would kill me on the way and stage an accident." Here Rommel made clear his belief that the Nazi government had already signed his death warrant, believing that any "trip to Berlin" was just a ruse to have him killed.

Rommel knew that they would come after him eventually, however, and on October 14th, 1944, two generals, Wilhelm Burgdorf, and Ernst Maisel, were sent to speak with Rommel. When the men arrived matters were cordial enough, but after exchanging pleasantries with Rommel's wife Lucia and his son Manfred, the men asked to speak with Rommel alone.

His wife and son then each went to their rooms upstairs, while Rommel spoke for about an hour with the generals. After speaking with the men Rommel then quietly went upstairs to see his wife. She would later recall that when her husband entered the room to see her, that there was a "strange and terrible expression on his face." When she asked him what was wrong, he replied, "I have come to say good-bye. In a quarter of an hour, I shall be dead."

He then informed her of how he was denounced by his colleagues as being a collaborator in the assassination plot, and Hitler had given him the choice of either turning himself in to be tried in court or to take the poison that the two men had been brought for just such an instance so that he could end his own life. Upon hearing this, Rommel's wife pleaded with him to throw himself on the mercy of the court.

She believed that there was still some possibility that he could vindicate himself. Rommel, however, refused, still believing that he would most likely be killed before he even arrived in Berlin. Rommel would ultimately agree to suicide, but he did so only on one condition: that he receive a pledge that his wife and son would not be harmed. The generals then informed Rommel that if he cooperated, his family would be taken care of, they would receive his pension, and he would even get a full state funeral, with the conspiracy charges never disclosed to the general public.

Despite the deceitful and twisted politics of Nazi Germany, the beaten and weary Erwin Rommel had no choice but to take these men for their word and agreed to take his own life in order to spare his family. After making his decision, Rommel was then led away to the men's car and drove out of sight. Approximately 25 minutes later the Rommels' phone rang, and a voice delivered the news, "A terrible thing has happened. The Field Marshal has had a hemorrhage in the car. He is dead."

Conclusion

After Rommel's forced suicide, the Nazi enforcers were true to their word; apparently content to put any charge of conspiracy against Rommel behind them, they kept up the charade, giving Rommel a state funeral with full military honors. The letters of condolences to the Rommel family then soon came flooding in, including one from Hitler directly to Rommel's wife Lucia that read, "Please accept my deepest sympathy on the loss of your husband. The name of Marshal Rommel will always be linked with the heroic fighting in North Africa."

The Nazis seemed almost to believe their own carefully crafted lies as they played the part and put on a show of mourning for the man that they had butchered. After all the pomp and circumstance that Nazi Germany could muster, Rommel was then finally cremated, and his ashes were sent to their final resting place in the small village of Harlingen, just a few miles west of Rommel's ancestral home of Ulm.

The legacy that Rommel leaves behind is mixed at best. He was, for most of World War Two, Hitler's top general, and by the simple virtue of his success, he was no doubt advancing the cause of Nazi ideology. Yet at the same time, Rommel often openly denounced the very same ideology that he was fighting for. Such a contradiction leads to some very conflicted views of the life and legacy of Field Marshal Erwin Rommel.

To some, he was simply just another Nazi, plain and simple, no better and no worse than all the other Nazis who threatened to lead the world into chaos. To others, Rommel was a brave soul who dared to stand up against Hitler's tyranny when the fear of the Nazi totalitarian state rendered most completely silent. For many more observers, there is a third option available when it comes to how Erwin Rommel should be perceived, however.

For them, Rommel is not entirely good or bad. He was simply a pragmatic soldier, trying to make the best of whatever situation he was placed in. This view would certainly fit his profile during his glory days in North Africa as the crafty Desert Fox, in the harsh sands of the Sahara with nothing but limited resources and his own cunning to get him through the day.

Rommel knew exactly what he needed in order to survive, and he used it. The same could be said for his actions against the Nazi system. It could be said that when he felt the Nazi regime benefited him and his country, he used it, but after the penetration of the Atlantic Wall and other disasters began to mount in 1944, the pragmatic side of Erwin Rommel told him to discard it.

This may be a more apathetic view of Rommel's motivations, but it could be successfully argued that his commitment to Nazi Germany rose and fell with its successes. For those that knew Rommel personally, they held him as a man of the highest honor, and one who would only do what he felt was right for his family and his country. In the end, regardless of your personal opinion, view, or bias, one thing can't be denied: the exploits of Field Marshal Erwin Rommel will live on for quite some time to come.

Printed in Great Britain
by Amazon